Traveller Education:
Changing Times, Changing Technologies

Ken Marks

On loan from:
The Traveller Team
Denewood Training Centre
Denewood Crescent
Bilborough, Nottingham NG8 3DH
Tel/Fax: 915 5758

Trentham Books
Stoke on Trent, UK and Sterling, USA

Trentham Books Limited

Westview House
734 London Road
Oakhill
Stoke on Trent
Staffordshire
England ST4 5NP

22883 Quicksilver Drive
Sterling
VA 20166-2012
USA

© 2004 Ken Marks

All rights reserved. No part of this publication may be reproduced or transmitted in any form or by any means, electronic or mechanical including photocopying, recording or any information storage or retrieval system, without prior permission in writing from the publishers.

First published 2004

British Library Cataloguing-in-Publication Data
A catalogue record for this book is available from the British Library

1 85856 351 8

Designed and typeset by Trentham Print Design Ltd., Chester and printed in Great Britain by Bemrose Shafron (Printers) Ltd., Chester

Acknowledgements

This report is an outcome of the research strand of the E-LAMP project. The project was also designed to promote a process of sharing, involving both teacher-practitioners and DfES colleagues. This proved a creative approach and makes it particularly important to acknowledge the numerous shared contributions which shaped some aspects of the research, as well as the role of the steering group in deciding priorities. Thanks are also due to the Nuffield Foundation for supporting the initiative and to Ludo Knaepkens, Marion Rowlands, Terry Waller and Gillian Klein for commenting on earlier drafts.

It has been a great privilege to work with the project and I have tried to reflect the ideas and concerns of others as accurately as I can. However it is important to add that the interpretations and recommendations expressed here don't necessarily reflect the views of the National Association of the Teachers of Travellers (NATT) which initiated the project.

Ken Marks, Research Associate
The Department of Educational Studies
The University of Sheffield.

Photographs

The photographs used on the cover of this report were supplied by EFECOT and by Traveller Education Services in: Cambridgeshire, Derby and Derbyshire, Durham and Darlington, Leicester, Leicestershire and Rutland, and Surrey

The E-LAMP steering group

The National Association of Teachers of Travellers (NATT) has a long tradition of seeking to improve services for Traveller children and of working with parent groups. So it is a great pleasure to endorse the comments and thanks expressed by the two parent representatives on the E-LAMP steering group (see forewords). The other members of the steering group were Anne Walker, Devon Consortium TES, Penny Lenton, Leicestershire, Leicester City and Rutland TES, and Ken Marks from the University of Sheffield.

Traveller mobility is a significant challenge for Traveller Education Support Services (TESS) and distance learning has evolved as one important part of the response. However, even the best of traditional materials and packs can leave young learners feeling unsupported and demotivated. E-LAMP has enabled an exploration of ICT and its potential to enhance distance learning. Our hope is that the work of the project will benefit Traveller children across all communities over time. When it ends, the groundwork established by the steering group will continue to be a platform from which NATT will seek to influence both policy and practice

Marion Rowlands (Avon Consortium TESS)
Chair of the E-LAMP Steering Group.

Contents

Forewords • iv
EXECUTIVE SUMMARY • v

SECTION 1 Introduction • 1
1.1 The underlying challenges • 2
1.2 Responses to mobility • 3
1.3 The project process • 4

SECTION 2 Gathering information • 5
2.1 ICT and Traveller Education Support Services • 5
2.2 ICT developments in parallel contexts • 11
2.3 Communication technology: a note on non-terrestrial options • 15

SECTION 3 Looking to future practice • 16
3.1 The primary sector and potential for immediate progress • 16
3.2 The secondary sector: some key issues for future development • 19

SECTION 4 Looking to policy for practice • 22
4.1 Moving forward • 22
4.2 Growth points and divides • 25

Notes • 28
References • 29

Forewords

As a child I travelled with my parents to fairs all over the Country. At each place we went to the local school, which we hated. Not the best way to receive an education. But it was the best my parents could do in the 50s. When I was invited to take part in the E-LAMP project as the Showmen's Guild representative, I felt this was the way forward at last for education on the move in the 21st Century. Using ICT to improve distance learning was new, innovative and a challenge for everyone. It has been a privilege to work alongside Ken Marks from the University of Sheffield, Marion Rowlands from NATT, the other members of the project steering group and the many teachers and families who have devoted their time. Also the important people from the DfES who have given their help – invaluable guidance and funding for a new project with laptops and datacards. Finally thank you to the Nuffield Foundation for enabling the E-LAMP project to come to fruition. In years to come I hope we shall look back with pride and say we were part of that.

Valerie Moody MBE, National Education Liaison Officer
The Showmen's Guild of Great Britain.

I would like to say thanks to the Nuffield Foundation for supporting this project and also to the steering group and the many committed teachers I have met. Circus families are among the most mobile in Traveller communities. Our children travel for nine months of the year, nearly every week in a different place. This project has explored ways to help us. We try to get our children into school when we can and some families have distance learning packs, but motivation is a problem. Now my son has been trialling a datacard and we can also keep in touch with his winter school and his friends no matter where we are. He doesn't feel so isolated and I'm sure when we go back in the winter he's going to find it much easier to settle down in his class. He's a boy, he hates writing. Now he does much more with his laptop and we also find resources on web-sites. It looks like laptops and datacards will be an important next step for all Circus children, and we hope that some of the other ideas which the E-LAMP project has investigated will open up even more effective ways of supporting our children in the future.

Kornelia Fossett, Moscow State Circus
Chair of the Circus Parents' Association

EXECUTIVE SUMMARY

This report is an outcome of a project supported by the Nuffield Foundation and co-ordinated by the National Association of the Teachers of Travellers (NATT), which came to be called E-LAMP, the 'E-Learning and Mobility Project'. As the name suggests, the project was concerned with developments in ICT which have opened the way for new forms of distance learning. The focus on mobility is specific to the needs of young Gypsy, Fairground and Circus Travellers, as many of these children spend part of their year on the move. Most of these children have a base-school, and part of the specialist role of LEA-based Traveller Education Support Services (TESS) is to work with schools and families to support distance learning. The main objective of E-LAMP was to explore ways in which ICT could enhance traditional paper-and-pack approaches to distance learning designed for these children. This report seeks to draw together the main findings of the research strand of E-LAMP in terms of information and issues. It also looks to the future and makes a series of recommendations related to both practice and policy. It includes a brief interim report of a derivative project called E-LAMP$_2$, and a parallel project in Leicestershire, both of which are currently exploring some ICT-enhanced work with Traveller children.

The information base

The project sought information in three key areas. How were TESS already using ICT to support their young learners? What could be gleaned from other developments which were using e-learning with children in out-of-school contexts? How best to bridge the communications gap between schools and mobile learners?

- The results of a national survey of the 96 TESS were supplemented by five case-study visits. The survey suggested that about one third of TESS were already beginning to use laptops in various contexts to support mobile Traveller pupils. But these were all small scale initiatives and there were frustrations about the lack of resources to develop work in this area. In ICT terms many TESS also felt marginalised within their LEAs. The case studies were a reminder of the wealth of good practice which has developed with traditional distance learning packs as well as some of the frustrations and limitations. ICT was mainly being used to enhance distance learning content, and as a way of helping children with the presentation of their work, but in one instance internet access was used to link learners to their base school and to web-based resources.

- Over a thousand children were found to be supported by their LEAs and receiving their 'schooling' at home via the internet. These included children with medical needs, and excluded pupils. There were four English service providers, although this number recently reduced to three following an amalgamation. A growing number of LEAs were pursuing these alternatives and relative cost, as compared with face-to-face provision, seems likely to have been a factor. The services providers were using a variety of approaches, some of which were more

- appropriate for mobile Traveller children than others. It was also possible to compare a Scottish initiative.
- Part of the reason why mobile Traveller children have not benefited from such developments is the challenge of non-terrestrial communication. The current realistic options were confirmed to be GPRS datacards, which use mobile telephone networks to link to the internet, and basic two-way satellite services.

Key issues and recommendations

A supplementary survey suggested that something of the order of 1200 mobile Traveller children currently receive some form of pack as an aid to the continuity of their learning whilst travelling away from their base-school. The challenge of non-terrestrial communication has clearly limited ICT developments in this area. However it also became apparent that there is some ambiguity in policy which originates from a focus on 'attendance' first expressed in the Children's Act of 1908. The *de facto* practice of TESS in supporting children who are out-of-school does not sit easily with current policy interpretations. Nor do mobile Traveller children have any entitlement to support, unlike children with medical needs and excluded pupils. **The project steering group recommends that this aspect of policy needs to be revised so that there is a solid platform for the development of ICT-based enhancement within a recognised and professional framework of responses to Traveller mobility.**

One of the issues which was evident from the case studies and related literature was the key role of parents in supporting distance learning in the mobile home environment. **The steering group recommends that future policy discussions about entitlement should also explore new forms of agreement with parents which celebrate partnership but also clarify obligations.**

Another key issue was the role of base-schools. There are particular concerns in the secondary sector where both logistics and attitudes are more problematic, reflecting more fundamental challenges. **The steering group recommends that the current base-school model should be consolidated and should remain central to ICT developments for primary age children, and welcomes DfES support for the new E-LAMP$_2$ project. The group also recommends the need for exploring blended ICT approaches for the secondary sector. These would draw on the evolving specialist services and look to new forms of partnership with TESS and base-schools.**

The supplementary survey also suggests that the vast majority of TESS outside greater London are supporting children with some form of pack. Distance learning is no panacea but the steering group would argue that it is an important part of the response to some patterns of Traveller mobility, and that ICT enhancement is particularly important as a way reinforcing home-school communication and reinforcing a sense of belonging and partnership. The interim evidence from E-LAMP$_2$ and Leicestershire certainly supports this view. Traveller education is always a challenging area, with progress achieved over time and often by example and localised experience. Individual TESS and base-schools will also vary in terms of their capacity to support new ICT developments. **From this perspective realistic growth points need to be encouraged and supported alongside and within the process of establishing a coherent framework, and resource implications should be taken into account.**

Introduction

The work of Traveller Education Support Services (TESS) is centred on bridging the gap between schools and Traveller communities. TESS seek to combat prejudice and raise awareness in schools, and to influence them in the direction of proactive sensitivity, whilst at the same time seeking to support and encourage Traveller families to engage with schooling. The importance of this part of the TESS remit was first highlighted by issues raised in the Plowden Report in 1967, and is reflected in literature which continues through to the most recent research and best practice publications (Bhopal *et al*, 2000, Bhopal 2004, Derrington and Kendall, 2004, and DfES, 2003). However, most TESS are also directly concerned with the challenge of Traveller mobility, a concern which may involve staff with outreach work, going out to work with children on site, and with distance learning support developed with the children's regular 'base-schools'.

The E-LAMP project was mainly concerned with distance learning and was funded by the Nuffield Foundation to address a specific challenge. Traditional paper-and-pack forms of distance learning have been used by TESS, working closely with base-schools, over a period of years. However, these have limitations which are even more evident for isolated young learners. This project set out to explore the potential for using ICT in this context, by drawing on experience from within TESS, including experience of European projects, and also from other initiatives which were already using e-learning to support children with medical needs and excluded or disaffected pupils. It also involved an assessment of the art of the possible in technological terms, as mobile children can't access the internet through the normal means of telephone lines or cable.

As the project developed a further challenge emerged. There have been frustrations within TESS about the failure of the DfES to give appropriate recognition to distance learning, and it became increasingly apparent that these concerns were not related simply to current limitations. Legislation dating from 1908, originally intended to respond flexibly to the needs of Traveller families and most recently reformulated within Section 444 of the 1996 Education Act, is still couched in terms of attendance and leaves TESS in an ambiguous situation. Supported distance learning has become an established part of *de facto* practice but is still not adequately recognised as a response which could form part of the foundation for a more effective approach to mobility.

Frustrations with a general lack of progress had also been echoed for some time at meetings between the National Association of the Teachers of Travellers (NATT) and representatives of the parents of both Fairground and Circus children. The composition of the project steering group reflects the joint nature of these concerns but it is important to note that the remit of E-LAMP was to address the needs of *all* mobile Traveller children. The proactive pressure had come directly from Fairground and Circus parents but the focus was inclusive.

This short report can't do full justice to the wealth of material gathered, but it offers an overview of the challenge, summarises evidence concerning existing experience (Section 2), and looks to future growth points (Section 3). Finally, it returns to the broader issues about policy and practice. Section 3 also includes a brief interim report on the progress of the derivative project, E-LAMP[2], which is targeted at the primary sector.

A note on terminology

For the purposes of this report the term 'Gypsy' is used to denote the Romany and Irish Traveller communities, together with similar traditional groupings. The term 'Traveller' is used in the generic sense to include both the Gypsy groupings and the Fairground and Circus communities.

1.1 The underlying challenges

The mobility patterns of families vary within and across communities. Typically a mobile Fairground or Circus family will be moving on a weekly basis during a travelling period from March/April through to October/November. Each Fairground family has a winter-base and its own annual 'run'. This will include setting up at fairs which are an established part of their route, where the family has rights to 'ground' within the structure of the 'Guild'[1], combined with flexible arrangements at other fairs and events. Travel patterns vary from regional to national. A small number of Fairground families also travel internationally. Circus families contract to one circus for the season, and travelling enterprises tend to move on a different circuit each year. Information from the Circus Parents' Association indicates a similar regional to countrywide spread, but with a bias towards national travel patterns and no automatic return to the same winter base.

The situation within the Gypsy communities is more complex and variable. Most families, but not all, have managed to establish a recognised home-base. Patterns also relate to economic opportunity. Travel is also influenced by traditional gatherings and sometimes by immediate family priorities and by enforced mobility. The Office of the Deputy Prime Minister (ODPM) research summary, based on the work of Niner (2003), reflects this variety and also suggests change over time.

> Frequency of travel ranges from full-time (mobile Gypsy) Travellers with no fixed abode, to families who live in one place most of the year. Some travel long distances across regions or even countries, whilst some regular (mobile Gypsy) Travellers never leave a single town.

> There are some indications that fewer ... now travel full time, and some have 'settled' for a combination of reasons ... However it would be unwise to assume that any trends towards greater 'settlement' is universal, or unidirectional. Individuals can pass from one pattern of travelling to another in line with family cycles, health and personal circumstances. (ODPM, 2003)

Some mobility is a response to seasonal work or other forms of activity which mean that a family can be at one location for a period of weeks. Other patterns are more fluid and are confounded by the lack of recognised transit sites. Here pressures to move on from unofficial stopping places have been exacerbated by the impact of the Criminal Justice and Public Order Act (1994) which means that families in transit face potential criminal prosecution. This problem is at its worst for something of the order of perhaps 1,500 families who have no established quarters and are forced into a transient lifestyle[2].

1.2 Responses to mobility

TESS in the UK pursue an integrated approach to the needs of traditional nomadic communities. This is unique within the European Union where any developments normally make a distinction between Gypsies and so called 'Occupational Travellers', a practice reinforced by the separate declarations of the European Council in 1989[3]. TESS are therefore equally concerned with the needs of Fairground and Circus families and Gypsy communities. This has the advantage of an holistic approach to traditions of nomadism, with lessons to be learned and shared within a context in which differences are also clearly recognised. From the perspective of TESS staff, prejudice and suspicion also form a common backcloth, and in the case of Fairground and Circus families seem to be rooted in reactions to a travelling lifestyle *per se* (Kiddle, 1999; Danaher, 2000).

Historically TESS have worked at developing a range of responses to mobility. In some instances families are encouraged to link with suitable local schools as they travel and the introduction of dual school-registration from January 1998 has eased this process (see, for example, O'Hanlon and Holmes, 2004: 50,51). Hopefully current developments based on a clearer understanding of the problems of inter-school mobility (Dobson *et al*, 2000) will help to make schools more sensitive to Traveller needs. DfES support for the *Red Book*, a family-held progress record system, also has the potential to reinforce inter-school continuity.

However school attendance is often impracticable or unhelpful for at least part of the travel period, particularly where families move on a frequent or relatively unpredictable basis. The secondary phase is especially daunting from the mobile perspective, with the prospect of a range of new teachers and approaches at every school visited, and different options and syllabi at Key Stage 4. Distance learning and outreach practices have developed as a response to these dilemmas, and in numerical terms these practices have gained more ground in the primary sector.

Distance learning is normally organised from the pupil's base-school with support from the appropriate TESS. It is currently most firmly established within the Fairground community. Projections from a national survey of English TESS[4], still in progress at the time of this report, are in line with figures from the community which suggest that 800 or so very mobile Fairground pupils, mostly of primary age, are travelling with packs. Estimates suggest that this is approximately half the current school-age mobile cohort. The projections also suggest a rather smaller number of Gypsy Traveller pupils with some form of pack, perhaps up to 400 in total, with the expected and considerable drop at secondary level. This latter total, of course, represents a small fraction of the potential mobile cohort. Discussions with TESS staff during the course of the project also indicate that Fairground children are more likely to be working within a distance learning structure, returning some work and receiving new work and feedback during the travel season, whilst responses to Gypsy children lean more towards independent learning packs that are designed for learning reinforcement with the possibility of return at the end of the mobile period. This seems to reflect less predictability and more fluid travel patterns, with the consequent problems for exchanging materials.

In the context of mobility, outreach involves peripatetic TESS staff, and sometimes small units, in going out to sites when families arrive in their area. Staff will encourage school attendance where realistic, will give support with any distance learning tasks, help to complete any records and may introduce new learning activities. Sadly, a limited version of outreach is often the only response for the 1,500 or so families with no recognised longer-term base and, as one commentator put it, teachers are then left trying to 'build on sand' (Evans, 1992).

1.3 The project process

The rest of this report is primarily concerned with practical and research outcomes and related recommendations. However it is important to appreciate something of the project process as this was integral to the direction and outcomes of the project. The original proposal to the Nuffield Foundation included a distinctive orientation towards dialogue and sharing. As well as seeking to gather information and explore issues in a systematic way, the project set out to bring practitioners together to exchange experiences, and also to seek to establish a constructive dialogue with the DfES.

In practice this integrated approach worked remarkably well. Three practitioner workshops were organised with support from Becta and these attracted an average of some 50 participants, including representatives from 39 of the 96 English TESS, with a core of about 20 represented at all three events. The DfES was also represented via the ICT in Schools team. The project was able to share ongoing research, and there were contributions from TESS which been involved with particular ICT initiatives. There were also practical inputs: the demonstration of a learning environment from the Nisai-Iris partnership (see below), a session on datacards supported by the mobile phone provider O_2, and another on web-based learning resources organised by Becta specialists. There were also contributions from other Traveller projects such as Cyberpilots, a web-based venture for Traveller children coordinated by the Friends and Families of Travellers (FFT). This process of dissemination and sharing was complemented by time set aside for participants to explore emergent issues at the first and third events, and these influenced the research agenda.

Discussions with the DfES, involving the Ethnic Minorities Achievement Project team directly responsible for Traveller education as well as the ICT in Schools team, were also productive and characterised by gathering momentum. The first meeting was exploratory, the second was more focused and in particular set the ground for the funding of the E-LAMP$_2$ initiative as well as highlighting some key issues, and the third was a valuable exchange embracing future policy and practice.

The activities of the project also reinforced the role of the new NATT ICT working group, set up in parallel with the project, which will now act as a forum and seek to build on progress to date.

Gathering information

The first phase of the E-LAMP project was weighted towards gathering information from three identified areas:

- Current experience of the use of ICT to support learning within TESS
- ICT developments specifically designed for distance learning in parallel out-of-school contexts, such as work with excluded pupils or those with medical needs
- Developments in non-terrestrial communication.

The snapshot formed during the first months of the project was then augmented and revised over the project year and the three subsections which follow attempt to collate overall findings.

2.1 ICT and Traveller Education Support Services

Ninety six TESS were identified, including a number of consortia. These TESS covered the majority of English LEAs[5]. A questionnaire exercise was used to inform an overall picture from these services and this was supplemented by five case studies, based on visits, interviews and related documentation. Interviews were recorded and visit summaries checked with participants.

The survey

As the newly formed NATT ICT working group had already drafted a questionnaire looking at staff-orientated ICT issues, it was agreed to combine approaches, and an enhanced schedule was designed and distributed to all Heads of Service. Sixty TESS responded (62%) but the level of return from the far north and north west was poor, perhaps reflecting lower NATT membership in those areas, and there was a 50% response rate from the Greater London region. Returns from the rest of England (the whole of the South, Midlands, East Anglia and Yorkshire as well as the conurbations between Manchester and Liverpool) were correspondingly higher with just over 80% coverage, and reflected a good balance between county and unitary LEAs. Subsequent information from some northern TESS suggest that the results of the survey give a fairly representative national picture.

Responses to questions directly related to the use of ICT with mobile Traveller children indicated that just over one third of TESS had been involved in some aspect of work to support pupils and this invariably involved the use of laptops. However the scale of this activity was low within individual TESS and comments indicated that efforts were frustrated by a lack of resources. Ten of the sixty respondents indicated that families had been able to borrow laptops from the TESS or occasionally from a base school. The laptops were intended to support distance learning but typically only two or three families were benefiting. Two other services were actively exploring similar loan possibilities. The Children's Fund was the most commonly mentioned source of funding, although some TESS had tried this route without success. Six TESS had been active in supporting work with families who had obtained their own laptops. Again numbers were very small and one TESS commented that even where parents were prepared and able to buy equipment the local base-schools did not seem ready to 'converse via ICT'.

The laptops were generally employed to help children to produce and present their work, but some TESS had provided the families with suitable CD ROMs as part of distance learning packs. Four of the respondents also mentioned some use, or attempted use, of email to support learning during the travelling season, focusing on potential links between learners and base schools and/or TESS staff. This included a funded initiative exploring the use of mobile phones as internet modems (see the Hertfordshire case study below), as well as efforts to encourage families to use ICT facilities in local libraries as they travelled.

Eleven respondents also indicated that service-owned laptops were sometimes taken out to support work with mobile families on sites. This included Circus, Fairground and unauthorised or transit Gypsy contexts. Again some comments suggested that efforts were limited by resource considerations.

Responses to broader questions about the use of ICT showed that many services have begun to use ICT to support their work in schools, and some have been involved with facilitating ICT courses at 16+, or providing training for Traveller parents. Others mentioned actual or planned site visits with mobile ICT units, via Connexions or other organisations. These were intended to raise awareness and/or offer taster training for adults.

The survey also generated some important contextual information. In particular, it showed the considerable range and diversity of services and roles, and a variable picture in terms of ICT staff training. TESS staffing can vary from a part-time support teacher through to a large team of colleagues with advisory, teaching and support

> The overall impression from this part of the survey exercise was of an increasing number of TESS exploring the potential for ICT as a means of supporting learning for children, conscious of the importance of raising awareness and developing skills amongst Traveller parents and adults, but frustrated by the lack of resources.

roles. Team structures and staffing levels have evolved over time and have been determined locally. The TESS responsibility is normally clear and separable but sometimes it is integrated within a team with a broader remit. These variations reflect different rationales, different levels and types of response to local Traveller needs and different LEA priorities. Such variations are important in the context of E-LAMP as staff time and focus are likely to influence the potential development of distance learning provision.

The questionnaire responses also suggested that most services had reasonable staff access to office-based computers, but with some notable exceptions and some particular issues relating to adequate internet access. Of wider concern, only 17 TESS (29% of respondents) reported 'good access' to ICT training and almost half had been excluded from the NOF training available to school-based teachers[6]. Some were never informed. Others were told that 'central services are not eligible', and in one instance the service was refused 'in spite of considerable efforts'. As one respondent commented, many services probably felt they were 'marginalised as usual'. Respondents were also asked to indicate their service priorities for ICT training and it was

> TESS were found to vary considerably in size, structure and linkage within LEAs. Access to ICT training was a fairly common concern, possibly indicating a lack of LEA awareness of the specific needs of staff working with Traveller children.

interesting to note that the improvement of ICT skills to develop more effective learning materials was ranked second in the list of popular choices.

The case studies

As noted above, the survey was supplemented by five case studies and these were intended to explore experiences, issues and emergent common themes. The first four were directly related to the use of ICT in distance learning and all were primarily, or exclusively, focused on initiatives with Showchildren. The fifth, undertaken later in the project cycle, was intended to counterbalance an increasing awareness that most successful distance learning activity had involved the Fairground community. This study therefore centred on the Durham and Darlington TESS as an example of an approach based on independent learning and developed for Gypsy children.

Two services, Derby and Derbyshire, and the West Midlands Consortium, were chosen because of their level of previous experience with European projects, coordinated by the European Federation for the Education of the Children of Occupational Travellers (EFECOT) and involving new technology[7]. Manchester was selected because of an innovative approach involving a local City Learning Centre (CLC) and Hertfordshire primarily to explore the supported use of internet communication, although this service had also benefited from involvement with an EFECOT project. In each case the service had originally developed distance learning as a response to Fairground families and relatively speaking, a smaller proportion of mobile Gypsy families had benefited from some form of pack-based approach. At the time of the studies 84 Fairground children and 63 Gypsy pupils were being supported via distance or independent learning resources across the four services. In each case the work had an important and distinctive place in a range of TESS activity which also reflected concerns with outreach and school attendance, and which involved support to far larger numbers of children and families.

These services had all looked to the potential of ICT to enhance distance learning and each was clearly building on a common ground of experience with traditional packs. There was a shared awareness of the importance of designing materials and activities which were tailored for individual pupils and suitable for self-learning, with built in teacher guidance. There was a recognition of the need to try to take account of travel patterns, and to consider realistic ways of exchanging completed work and new materials wherever practicable. There was encouragement for families to link up with other TESS as they travelled, to support work with the packs. There was a strong emphasis on involving parents as partners in the process, both through preparatory and review meetings and through encouragement to keep in touch with base schools and/or their own TESS. The services offered a wealth of experience and some had developed their own guidelines. The West Midlands Consortium had also been involved with a European project which had published a comprehensive guidance manual (EFECOT, 1994).

Some important issues were recognised across the board. Clearly the intention is to build on the child's experience at their base school, but schools had varied in their commitment or capacity to produce suitable materials and to provide support. Where partnership had developed, there were some excellent examples of good whole-school practice but often a relatively fragile dependence on one or two key members of staff. This could be even more critical for secondary schools, where the logistics of distance learning support were much more complex. These TESS had therefore been involved in a range of approaches with their base schools. Schools at one end of the spectrum had come to see the provision of distance learning as part of their inclusive role with the TESS as a partner in the process. At the other end, the TESS would have to work at gathering basic ideas and information from school and take on most of the responsibility for developing materials and providing ongoing support.

These TESS also acknowledged the motivational problems faced by their young distance learners. During the travel season the trailer home was also the busy centre of family life and work, with plenty of distractions. Parental encouragement was felt to be critical, but delays in feedback and, perhaps worse, sorting out misunderstandings, made such encouragement more difficult and children tended to complete less work over time. As children became older materials tended to be more text-based and specialised and this could create problems for parents who wanted to offer support but had missed out on schooling themselves. Secondary schooling posed particular problems as children became young adults within their communities and the relevance of schooling could become a major issue.

Each of these services had looked to ICT as a way of developing materials to stimulate and encourage self-learning activity as well as a potential way of helping to bridge the communication gap. Involvement with European projects had also stimulated progress within three of the services. Staff who had developed or used selected learning software talked about the way in which good animated or interactive materials had 'caught the children's imagination'. Children had also responded positively to the 'professional feel of on-screen materials', and the value was recognised of interactive reinforcement exercises which gave immediate corrective feedback. However there was a strong commitment to a balanced approach, combining computer-based learning with aspects of traditional packs and reinforcing the role of books, handwriting and practical tasks. EFECOT project experiences had also suggested that it was valuable to use the 'computer-as-teacher': using the computer interface to take the lead in presenting the programme of work to be done, with guidance about the use of specific software and/or parts of the pack to complete suggested learning activities. On a more cautionary note, there was a salient reminder about the amount of time needed to select and develop suitable ICT-based materials, and a parallel concern about staff expertise within base-schools and TESS.

Two of the services had also had successful experience of using ICT to reinforce communication. In a sense they offered experience from the extreme ends of a spectrum, but both gave important and complementary messages. The Hertfordshire service had currently been working with a local comprehensive, the John Warner School, to explore the use of email to support two secondary Fairground pupils, with mobile phones as modems linking the learner

> Each of these TESS had a distinctive focus on supporting distance learning and had considerable experience in this field. Each stressed the importance of parental involvement. Each had developed a flexible approach to base schools: aiming at the ideal but responsive to local possibilities and constraints and aware of additional challenges for secondary schooling. Each had also looked to ICT to enhance work with packs, but within a balanced approach and with concerns about the additional time and skills required to develop suitable materials.

laptops to the internet. This venture has been written up (Meadows and Stockdale, 2003). Although small scale, it signals a significant breakthrough based on the systematic use of simple and available technology, with success perhaps best revealed in the words of two pupils quoted in the report:

> I found the computer work really easier than a paper-based pack because I could email (it) ... as soon as I did it ... I could have my work marked and I could see if there was anything I needed to cover more promptly

> The emailing has been good because the school knows I have been doing my work ... I can send it back to them and it doesn't take ages. They can email me new work and help me with things I am stuck on

The learning programme was primarily focused on History and included structured computer-based tasks as well as more exploratory work in which the pupils were asked to make use of web-based resources. Both internet access and messaging had clearly added significantly to the distance learning experience. The initiative had also focused attention on developing a whole school approach, putting the materials on the website as a resource for all pupils, including, as the report notes, any pupils who are 'away from school, for example, students away due to illness, exclusion or extended family visits'.

The other example of enhanced communication stems from the participation of the West Midlands Consortium in a project funded by the European Space Agency (ESA) and coordinated by EFECOT with trials during 2000. Trapeze was at the time a leading-edge technological project designed to explore a new approach to two-way satellite communication. The project developed a suitable learning environment which allowed children to access a new 'lesson' each day, and provided both email and chat room facilities. Ten English Fairground pupils were involved, along with ten Fairground children from the Netherlands. The children's ages ranged from eight to thirteen, with the English children all at KS2. Two members of staff from the consortium were involved in preparing some imaginative interactive materials, training and preparing the families and acting as tutors during the trials. This project proved successful and was written up and evaluated for ESA (Vanbuel *et al*, 2000). Significantly, the children experienced a virtual classroom environment. They worked on-line each morning knowing that their tutors were immediately available for help and advice. Completed work was returned at the click of a button and could be checked and feedback ready the next day. Tutors were also able to modify, supplement and tailor lessons in the light of each child's progress. Some of the evaluative comments from pupils can be

> Both these initiatives clearly demonstrate the significant potential of improved learner-tutor dialogue to support distance learning. The Trapeze project was also significant in showing what can be achieved through an integrated learning environment, c.f. the initiatives discussed in the next section.

seen to resonate with the more recent feedback from Hertfordshire:

> It was great to know how many I got in maths ... and what mistakes I made. When I do the ordinary (pack) work I don't know how well I have done for a week or even longer

> If I was stuck ... there was someone there who could help me without having to wait days or even weeks

Others comments reflected the potential of a designed environment. As one parent put it: 'it was like having a classroom in your home ... with the teacher there every day'

The Trapeze trials were short but successful. They highlighted other issues, most notably the significant amount of time needed by staff acting as tutors, and a new dimension of preparation for families as well as pupils.

Parental preparation was emphasised by all four case study participants, but the need for supportive ICT skills added a new dimension to the task. The Manchester Service had organised a course for Traveller parents at the CLC as a prelude to five of the children going off with laptops and materials, whilst the other TESS had all been involved in training initiatives with their parents. Apart from developing supportive technical skills, parents were reported to have taken a renewed interest in their children's learning, and some fathers became involved for the first time. A small number of families had gone on to purchase their own computers and some parents had sought further ICT training. Pupil preparation also needed to cover the ICT dimension, and two respondents commented that this added a new layer to the variety of base-school relationships, that is, the dependence on the level of ICT development in the school.

Durham and Darlington

The visit to Durham and Darlington was added to the original schedule in order to explore experience with Gypsy families. The major part of the work of the service was reported to be focused on supporting and encouraging schooling for some 700 Gypsy pupils. Most of the families were permanently housed or settled on authorised sites but about 200 had a semi-nomadic lifestyle and were the focus for packs designed with an independent learning orientation. Developing the work with packs had had to be built over time, while focused efforts were made to reinforce regular attendance at base-schools. Significant progress had been made through the use of two specialist and pro-active bridging posts. The eventual target for the service is that every mobile child should have a pack, and in the previous year 63 primary and 17 secondary pupils had benefited, along with 15 pre-school children. The close relationship between bridging activity and packs has, sadly, been demonstrated by a dip in both attendance and the realistic potential for packs due to the recent withdrawal of LEA support for the specialist Darlington-based post.

The independent learning ethos had developed partly as a response to the practicalities of exchanging work during travel periods. Children were only asked to bring their work back when they returned to base. However return rates had always been low, of the order if one in six. The balance of responsibility for producing materials, school/TESS, had also been an issue and these concerns had led to a European-funded initiative to look at whole-school approaches to independent learning, with materials which could be used in the classroom and for any child to continue in any interrupted learning situation. Guidelines and exemplar materials were produced for the primary sector (Durham and Darlington TES, 2001) and have proved popular across a number of local primary schools. Starting the process in school is clearly an advantage for Traveller pupils. There is a strong emphasis on the language and ethos of independent learning and on self-assessment, and work is parallel to tasks within school.

The intention is to encourage similar integrated developments in secondary schools and the visit included discussions at Eastbourne Comprehensive school in Darlington where a member of TESS staff is working with the school to pioneer independent learning materials within the English Department. The Eastbourne initiative is also central to future TESS thinking about the use of ICT. Once materials are piloted the intention is to produce an interactive CD-ROM version, as well as looking to the potential for email to link learners to school and possibly the school intranet. In the long term this could enable something closer to supported distance learning but the emphasis on integrated approaches and on independent learning skills will remain central.

> The experience of the Durham and Darlington TESS is a reminder of the continuing importance of bridging roles in the long-term development of effective provision for large numbers of Gypsy children. The emphases on independent learning skills and whole-school approaches are creative responses to current realities and they resonate with some of the best distance learning practice from the other case-studies.

2.2 ICT developments in parallel contexts

The previous section illustrates a wealth of experience of distance learning developed within TESS, often stretching back many years and including some experience of innovative European projects aimed at developing ICT-based approaches. It is an irony that actual developments in this country have been stimulated by other groups of children who are affected by interrupted schooling. This partly reflects the challenge of non-terrestrial communication, but perhaps also the relative invisibility of this aspect of the work of TESS within and across LEAs as well as the ambiguity of the status of distance learning provision for English Traveller pupils.

Part of the E-LAMP remit was to look at such parallel developments, to compare approaches and structures and to see what could be learned and applied. The exercise was initiated with recommendations from Becta and finally honed in on three main ICT-based initiatives in England, together with one Scottish pilot project. Each of these was visited and the commentary contained in this section is based on discussions, available documentation, and where practicable, demonstrations. A new initiative, 'Vu2 education', emerged during the course of the year and in this instance information is based on documentation, telephone discussion and a brief on-line trial.

At the time details were originally sought, Satellite School was a registered charity coordinated from Leicestershire offering an internet-based service for 100 children with medical needs, drawn from nine LEAs. This initiative has now been integrated within the Nisai-Iris structure (see below) and at the time of writing is still available in its original form. Notschool.net is coordinated from Ultralab (Anglia Polytechnic University). Extensively funded by the DfES, it currently offers a web-based learning service for excluded and disaffected pupils as well as other children who have become disengaged from school. During 2003 some 480 pupils were registered and it was offering a service to thirteen English LEAs plus Jersey. Both pioneering ventures date back to the late 1990s and both offer well established asynchronous approaches. In each case children join what is effectively a single, and potentially national, structure.

The third initiative, Nisai-Iris, is a more recent development which started with a different rationale. The approach has its roots in a joint venture between Warwickshire LEA and a commercial provider which set out to resource and support a two-part learning environment, one part synchronous, i.e. with tutors and learners on line at the same time, and the other asynchronous. At the time information was sought, nineteen LEAs were reported to be involved in the resource partnership. About half were active, in the sense of providing services for out-of-school children. Something of the order of 300 children were reported to be using the system. As originally conceived, the central team provides a service, but each LEA employs its own local tutors and can tailor the use of the twin environments to local needs and preferences. The initiative started as a response to children with medical needs, but now emphasises the potential for integrated approaches which can offer LEA services to all out-of-school children. There is also an emphasis on combining the use of the environments with face-to-face activity where this is practicable and felt to be in the best interests of the children. Satellite School, now renamed Nisai Satellite School, has recently been incorporated as the basis for a national structure which will build on the strengths of the original concept. This means that LEA partners will have the option to develop and staff mixed approaches locally or to enrol pupils in what is planned to become a broader concept, the Nisai Virtual Academy.

This integrated local rationale also characterises the Glasgow-based SchoolsOut project which has just completed its pilot phase (Spring, 2004) and has offered a service for any child in an 'interrupted learning' situation with a blended use of virtual and face-to-face learning contexts. The LEA target is to provide a service for up to 40 pupils.

The final project, Vu2educate, is an emergent initiative being developed by Vu2 Media Ltd with support from NESTA (The National Endowment for Science, Technology and the Arts). This is a centralised initiative featuring scheduled lessons with a live tutor, email linkage and interactive activities. Lessons are broadcast by internet to small differentiated groups of about ten learners and these are followed up by a programme of on-screen learning with access to archived lesson materials. At present 22 LEAs are reported to have become involved at some level and early work has serviced some 150 pupils.

This overview demonstrates that the internet is being used to provide distance schooling, in the home context, for a substantial and growing number of out-of-school pupils and with interest from a significant number of LEAs. However the focus of these initiatives is currently on developing approaches and materials for secondary pupils[8]. In one sense this is frustrating, as the obvious growth point for Traveller education is at primary level. But it does offer the possibility of some radical new thinking about the secondary challenge.

It is not possible to offer a full description of each of these ventures nor of a rounded comparative critique in this short report. However it does seem important to try to pick out some comparative features which have direct relevance to the Traveller context and this requires some all-too-brief thumbnail sketches.

(Nisai) Satellite School

The Satellite School approach is centralised and has been firmly based on developing materials for the National Curriculum and GCSE requirements. Tutor-developed worksheets are tailored for individual learners and draw on a bank of resources. These include selected textbooks, CD-ROMS and video tapes. Tasks can also require learners to access recommended websites. Work was originally exchanged as email attachments but the exchange is now incorporated into a learning environment which will be enhanced by on-line activities within the new Nisai-Iris structure. The system is designed to work at normal telephone modem speeds

The Nisai-Iris Partnership

The Nisai-Iris approach took the Key Stage 3 National Curriculum as its starting point, with Key Stage 4 to follow. It plans to facilitate flexibility through programme choices, the creative use of its twin environments and the potential to build a blended approach including face-to-face activity. The twin environments facilitate (a) timetabled classroom sessions for small groups of typically six learners, using an established product, Learnlinc, with audio, text messaging, whiteboard and shared application options, as well as (b) asynchronous individual learner activity within a structure with a developing range of materials, tasks and interactive exercises. This system, too, is currently designed for telephone modem transfer capacity.

Vu2educate

As noted above, the new Vu2educate is a centralised initiative which currently offers timetabled and live broadcast sessions. The tutor uses audio communication, the sessions are planned around interactive exercises and there is a dedicated two-way email link during lessons. The initial emphasis is on Key Stage 4 and the service is currently offering courses for Maths, English, ICT and Science. Each session finishes with an interactive on-screen task sheet which is effectively the basis for an asynchronous programme for pupils, with work to be returned to the tutor. There is also access to archived lesson materials and there are plans to develop a full environment to support the asynchronous part of the learning process. The broadcast materials require broadband connection.

SchoolsOut

This is a local LEA initiative which offers a flexible and blended approach, part of which is an asynchronous service drawing on two established resources: Learn Premium, itself a full materials-orientated environment designed for the Scottish curriculum, and Plato, an integrated learning system aimed at improving numeracy and literacy skills support. There is also a linked communal area where learners and tutors can interact and share. The system is designed for cable or ADSL telephone speeds but with back-up that uses normal telephone modem rates.

Notschool.net

Here the environment is the hub of a centralised learning approach. It is asynchronous and is distinctive in its emphasis on the learner and the community, rather than being syllabus-led. The structure is based on a customised version of the First Class environment and the rationale is constructivist, with the challenge of supporting the learner in the pursuit of active and self-regulating goals (see, for example, Elen, 1996: 75-77 and Jonassen *et al*, 1999: 7-11). Learners ('researchers') are encouraged to develop their own programme based on a wide and fluid range of existing topic options and their own expressed interests, and are facilitated by personal tutors ('mentors'), as well as subject specialists ('experts') who help develop materials and activities, and other researchers. Support is also offered by 'buddies', now drawn from the ranks of ex-researchers. The approach and structure are more fully described in recent reports (Duckworth, 2003 and Notschool.net, 2003). The content is media rich and relies on ADSL or IDSN connections.

Some comparisons

These brief thumbnail sketches give enough background to draw out three important comparative issues. One is of a practical nature and is outlined here, as it relates directly to the mobile context. The others are more fundamental. The first involves blending, the combination of virtual experiences with face-to-face learning, and raises direct questions about the potential role of base schools. This is discussed in Section 3. The second is broader and concerned with both the nature of the curriculum and with pedagogy, and is discussed in Section 4. These latter issues are potentially of importance for the primary sector but are arguably critical for the secondary sector, and it is here that these ICT-based distance learning initiatives are currently evolving.

The immediate contextual issue relates to synchronicity and here it is important to distinguish between three separate scenarios. Some environments rely on real-time interchanges between tutors and learners. The Vu2 initiative and the Learnlinc part of the Nisai-Iris approach are examples of this. Other developments have the potential for slots where particular staff are available on line at set 'classroom' times, but the work is essentially asynchronous. This was also the approach used in Trapeze. Finally there are environments which are fully asynchronous, with tutors and learners working flexibly but sometimes with a degree of generally supportive tutor presence. Models which rely on real-time exchanges would be problematic for many mobile learners, with their differing transit patterns. However, the other two approaches are viable and it is interesting to note that a current Dutch environment coordinated by the Stichting Rijdende School (SRS) for Fairground children mirrors Trapeze in using a set-time classroom approach, and with learners expected to 'attend' unless the family is on the move. From this perspective, variations of the asynchronous options offered by the Nisai-Iris, Nisai Satellite School and Notschool.net each offer suitable alternatives for the mobile context.

2.3 Communication technology: a note on non-terrestrial options

The ICT-based approaches discussed so far all seek to combine some of the strengths of computer-based learning activity with terrestrial communication (phone lines and cable) in order to give access to learning environments and the internet. Interestingly, none of these pioneer developments had considered the needs of very mobile home learners and none had considered the additional challenge of providing services via non-terrestrial communication. Indeed one of the benefits of E-LAMP has been to raise the visibility of the challenge.

For the purposes of the project four non-terrestrial approaches were explored. Two of these, GPRS datacards[9] and two-way satellite options, are currently commercially available and essentially provide channels for internet communication. The other two were investigated because of their availability, or potential availability, to Traveller families. Here hand-held devices were of interest because of their portability and interactive TV because the satellite delivery of digital TV is ubiquitous.

Both GPRS datacards and handheld devices use mobile telephone networks. The Learning and Skills Development Agency is currently exploring the use of both mobile phones and hand-held computer devices as learning support tools and one TESS is involved in the m-learning pilot trials. However limited screen sizes are a clear constraint and this option seems more likely to be useful as a motivational tool and for providing learning reinforcement. The use of datacards which slot into a laptop to provide wireless access to the internet, offers more promise. Datacards were known to be in use in the Netherlands for the SRS initiative with Fairground learners, but cost and UK coverage had been seen as problematic. Discussions with the East Midlands Broadband Consortium, which had experimented with coverage, and subsequent explorations of pricing for groups of learners, allayed these concerns. However datacards only support low bandwidth, and in terms of overall UK coverage this is likely to remain the situation, certainly for the medium term. There are also potential problems with synchronous distance learning applications as actual transfer rates are variable, depending on traffic volumes.

As noted above, two-way satellite communication is also commercially available. Coverage is more robust, bandwidths are higher and one of the English TESS had been involved in the successful European pilot, Trapeze. On the other hand, user costs are relatively high and families have to transport, set up and tune in the dish every time they move.

Digital satellite TV has the advantage that it has become part of life for many Traveller families. However, fully interactive satellite TV, with two way communication and which can access some forms of internet-based activity, currently uses a terrestrial, low bandwidth, return link. Given the limited size of the potential market, expert opinion seems to be that it is unlikely that return satellite links or satellite/mobile-phone developments will emerge. Digital TV does in itself offer a wealth of educational resources which can be targeted as supplementary material in distance learning programmes, but this is likely to remain its potential contribution for mobile Traveller children.

3 Looking to future practice

The evidence from Section 2 of this report indicates a wealth of experience of independent and distance learning across TESS, but with the acknowledgement of the limitations of traditional learning packs and a readiness to explore the benefits of ICT enhancement. It also acknowledges the increased challenge posed for secondary age pupils, and projections from the current E-LAMP2 survey suggest that less than 30% of all packs issued are for this age group.

This section is concerned with looking to ICT developments as potential growth points for Traveller children, some more immediate than others. Here both the Traveller and base-school contexts, and the current options suggest a distinction between the primary and secondary sectors. Each is considered in turn.

3.1 The primary sector and potential for immediate progress

The evidence suggests that TESS have a strong commitment to working with primary base-schools and partnership has characterised some of the best practice with traditional packs. There seems to be a good case for beginning to build on this approach by using ICT to enhance both learning activities and communication, particularly in the absence of other immediately suitable developments targeted at this age group.

Well designed ICT-based materials can in themselves have an impact on motivation, a significant factor for isolated learners. However, the communication gap is arguably more fundamental and this is reflected in the concept of 'transactional distance' as developed by Moore (1993). Moore's critique of traditional distance learning approaches was concerned with the psychological, rather than geographical, space between tutor and learner. He drew attention to two factors which impact on this conception of distance. One concerns the potential for tutor-learner dialogue, the other the degree of flexibility and responsiveness of the distance learning programme to emerging learner needs. As demonstrated by the TESS initiative in Hertfordshire, the internet can immediately enable more effective feedback and supportive dialogue. It also allows tutors the flexibility to modify work, for example by sending simple attachments or referring pupils to new web resources. In Moore's terms the internet is a powerful tool for reducing the psychological gap.

Moore also highlighted the potential impact of learner autonomy on transactional distance (*ibid*), an important reminder that ICT-based solutions are no immediate panacea. As other authors have explored Moore's framework in the light of developments in e-learning, they have suggested that the level of learner ICT skills should itself be considered as another factor affecting the transactional distance between learner and tutor (for a discussion related to web-based environments see Chen, 2001). So with potential comes a new set of demands and this reinforced the steering group view that it would be important to move forward on a pilot basis, building ICT into the established pack approach. This suggested a model similar to the one pioneered in Hertfordshire, but taking the opportunity to use dedicated GPRS datacards rather than mobile phones as modems. As discussions had already been initiated it was possible to explore this option with the DfES, and one important outcome of the original project is a new initiative named E-LAMP$_2$ to emphasise its derivative nature, which started in February 2004, and will run through to the end of the main travelling season. The new initiative also sparked a similar project in Leicestershire

E-LAMP$_2$ and Leicestershire: a brief interim report

The E-LAMP$_2$ initiative was agreed in December 2003, with substantial support from the DfES and contributions from The Showmen's Guild of Great Britain, and later from the NASUWT and the mobile phone provider O$_2$. O$_2$ has also provided technical and administrative back up. Four TESS and base-school partnerships are involved

- Bolton TESS (working with Bolton Parish Church School)
- Surrey TESS (working with Lingfield Primary School)
- The Avon Consortium TESS (working with St John's Mead Primary School)
- Cambridgeshire TESS (working with Wilburton Village Primary School)

Each family has been loaned a laptop and a datacard with a monthly mobile phone allowance. Each family also has a combined printer/scanner unit and an individualised selection of CD-ROMs and other software chosen by their schools and intended to enhance pack-based learning. Each school has funding for a half-a-day staff cover to release appropriate teachers.

Given the rationale of the project, one requirement was that participating base schools should have a minimum of four, and ideally five, KS2 pupils with experience of using distance, rather than independent, learning packs. This emphasis has in practice meant that Fairground children are pioneering the approach. The initiative in Leicestershire has a similar rationale and is running in parallel. It has proved a useful complement as it is working with schools which have very small numbers of Fairground children with packs, typically one or two, and is also piloting some work at the secondary level. The E-LAMP$_2$ project is now also using back-up equipment to support two secondary pupils, one from the Circus community which has its own distinctive challenges, and one from an Irish Traveller family with direct support from a TESS rather than school. This means that 30 children are participating in trials, with 24 from the primary sector and six of secondary age.

Progress to date indicates that datacards are proving effective in supporting travel patterns. Coverage has generally been good throughout the country, although with some localised communication blackspots in rural areas. Data transfer rates, which depend on the overall amount of GPRS traffic using the network, have been generally 'good' or 'satisfactory', but variable with location and sometimes time of day. The interim feedback suggests that coverage and transfer rates have caused some frustrations but that overall experience is positive in spite of these experiences[10].

The approach has been more effective where TESS and base-schools were able to adopt an integrated, rather than complementary, approach to training and follow up; with proactive encouragement, for example by mobile phone, during the early weeks of family travel periods. Email exchanges and the more fluid approach to

> If there is a problem we can email the school and ask for help. Contact is much quicker (*parent*)
>
> She likes to get emails from school. Makes her feel she's not forgotten (*parent*)
>
> (Attachments are)....changing ways of doing work (*pupil*)
>
> I know if I've done it correctly, and [I know] quickly (*pupil*)
>
> My friends and me have been keeping in touch about where we are going next and stuff like that (*pupil*)
>
> It makes them feel that someone is looking at what they've done (*parent*)

materials both raise new demands. It is therefore no surprise to find that dedicated time and a clear focus for ongoing support within base schools and/or TESS is also emerging as a crucial success factor.

It isn't yet possible to give a balanced overview of the impact of the initiatives, but there are some interesting threads within the early feedback. Email is being used for contact with staff and for schoolwork, but also in some instances with classmates or named 'buddies' within school, and there is a sense of still belonging rather than, as one member of staff put it, 'out of sight, out of mind'. Comments from parents and pupils reflect responses from Hertforshire and Trapeze pupils as well as this sense of awareness of school.

There are indications that motivation has improved and that both software and websites are enriching the process. In some families the children are also reported to be more committed to work with their traditional packs, as well as their tasks with laptops, and this again seems to relate to the enhanced awareness of school.

It is important to add that these are early days, that novelty may well be a factor and that progress has been variable across schools and families. It will also be important to evaluate progress in terms of current attainment levels, particularly for children who are below age-related targets or have learning support needs. There seems little doubt that the approach will demonstrate that internet-based developments have an important part to play for some children, but with broader questions about how they should fit within a flexible, more effective and recognised framework for supporting these young distance learners (see Section 4). For now the last word should rest with some of the young learners.

> I like the laptop a lot. I like to rite storys. I like the maths games a lot. I like to rite letters to my frens. (*email*)
>
> ... instead of homework being a chore it has been something to look forward to, a laptop has definitely improved my homework standards (*extract from a written pupil feedback exercise*)
>
> The weather is really bad here today so I'm staying inside with mum and doing my schoolwork. I've just got some reading left to do now then I can go and play with my ferret (*email*)

3.2 The secondary sector: some key issues for future development

Clearly there are some exemplary secondary schools, like John Warner School in Hertfordshire, which have an inclusive rationale and the commitment to develop ICT-based approaches over time. It is also pleasing to see secondary pupils included in the current datacard trials. Such initiatives are to be welcomed and encouraged. However there are question marks about the role of secondary base-schools which seem all too pertinent to many, perhaps most, of them. The evidence collated from the case studies made reference to the logistical challenges. The subject-specialist nature of secondary delivery means that the whole process of preparing suitable materials, exchanging packs and offering support has always been more complex, and progress made has often been all too dependent on one or two key members of staff rather than forming part of a whole school ethos. ICT offers new opportunities but doesn't resolve these problems. Indeed enhanced communication could be seen to add to the logistical dilemma in the busy school environment.

The emergence of the new ICT-based approaches described in Section 2 would seem to offer alternative, and potentially more effective, ways ahead for mobile Traveller pupils. All of them offer structured and relatively sophisticated ways of addressing transactional distance. All use specialist distance learning tutors and materials, and each has developed learning approaches for the virtual context. Some of them also offer scope for blended approaches, which could involve base-schools and TESS in new forms of partnership. Others are centralised which would make partnership more difficult, and in the case of Notschool.net any involvement from base-schools or TESS staff would be specifically precluded. Here the current view of the scheme coordinators is that the effectiveness of their particular approach is entirely dependent on not pursuing blended possibilities with other educational partners.

This stance is not based on comparative evidence but it raises important questions, as Notschool.net is working successfully with a range of disaffected pupils. Disaffection is a key issue for large numbers of secondary-age Traveller pupils. A separated orientation might well have its attractions. On the other hand TESS staff have critical bridging roles. Strengthening distance learning within blended approaches, with base-schools as partners, albeit with important lessons to be learned from Notschool experience, could also affect the schools positively themselves.

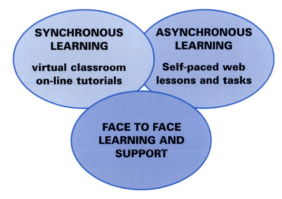

A blended approach can combine face-to-face learning and e-learning

The E-LAMP steering group therefore took the view that, for the purposes of the project, it was important to prioritise an exploration of blended approaches which could address the distance learning challenge but also support new and creative relationships. Two options were considered as the basis for possible trials. The first of these builds on integrated LEA ventures. The second is more radical and looks to the establishment of new regional structures for Traveller pupils involving staff from both Traveller services and base-schools.

The integrated LEA rationale was investigated by extending the Derbyshire TESS case study to include joint discussions with the TESS and the Derbyshire Virtual Community, part of the Nsai-Iris partnership that is currently providing services for excluded pupils and pupils with medical needs. These are essentially separate services but draw on the strengths and experience of a common staff team. The service for children with medical needs is entirely based on the asynchronous option, whereas work with excluded pupils also uses the synchronous environment and has a face-to-face element. Disapplication (not being constrained to the whole of the National Curriculum) is used creatively and the team has developed a range of expertise with both motivated and disaffected learners. There would also seem to be a good platform for linking with potential base-school learning and drawing on the supportive role of TESS. An asynchronous service could be offered that used datacards, but two-way satellite would clearly offer more secure communication and could also offer some supportive use of the synchronous environment, provided this was an optional rather than essential feature.

The regional approach was also investigated by extending part of case study discussions, in this instance with the West Midlands Consortium TESS which provides a coordinated service across fourteen LEAs. As this would be a new structure, these discussions centred on ways of staffing and organising, drawing on current TESS and base-school teachers and including the use of part-secondment to virtual tutor roles. Given current levels of cooperation between the TESS and base-schools across the region there seems to be a realistic foundation on which to build. Other English TESS are within regional structures which could also form the basis for parallel approaches, although these structures are currently mainly a means of sharing experience.

Both of the models considered building on partnership with base-schools. The first model is localised and offers a more immediate type of growth point, but only for the children within LEAs which become partners in a suitable integrated scheme. Currently Nisai-Iris offers the only viable basis for trials. The second model involves new structures which would need to link with a service facilitator, again like Nisai-Iris, and be built over a period of time. It could offer a more comprehensive service, one rooted more firmly within Traveller cultures and within the TESS legacy.

The alternatives involve both practical considerations and value judgments, but the steering group would argue that there is certainly a case for investing in trials with one or both blended models in order to gain experience. On the other hand this argument raises issues about cost and sustainability. The per-pupil cost of an approach like E-LAMP$_2$ is around £1,000; taking account of equipment depreciation, communication costs and an allowance for staff time within school. The cost for a secondary pilot using specialist staff working with the Nisai-Iris environment was calculated to be of the order of

£6,000, or £7,500 if satellite communication is used instead of datacards. Where information was available, the emerging costs of a pupil 'place' with one of the existing distance learning services range from £4,000 to £6,000. This is a complex area, particularly for blended approaches, and there are hidden subsidies which suggest that it is probably safer to make longer term plans based on the upper end of the cost range.

These cost levels raise concerns about the dangers of proceeding with pilot projects which, even if successful, raise expectations but are not consolidated. Sustainability, in turn, seems inextricably linked to policy and to notions of entitlement, as well as recognition of the (currently *de facto*) status of distance learning support for mobile Traveller children. These are also issues for the development of parallel work within base schools, including primary base schools. The costs of new approaches to the secondary challenge simply serve to highlight the issues. The final section of this report therefore argues that policy and practice will need to develop in parallel.

4 Looking to policy for practice

Educational systems which have evolved for sedentary populations do not fit well with nomadic lifestyles. The suggestion that nomadism and school attendance are not incompatible, written from the European perspective (Liégeois,1998: 100), highlights the need for school responsiveness if understood in general terms. However Liégeois also acknowledged the need for other approaches which 'recognise the reality of nomadism' (Liégeois,1998: 269) and this rationale has also been central to the European work of EFECOT (see below). In the English context, the recent emphasis on inter-school mobility is to be welcomed in terms of responsiveness (DfES, 2003a, 2003b), but can also be seen as a mixed blessing. There is a real danger that the attendance and inter-school rationale will draw attention away from some of the realities of *Traveller* mobility and leave essential parts of the challenge, as seen from the perspective of TESS and families, unaddressed. From their perspective there is a case for basing both policy and practice on the grounded reality of mobile Traveller lifestyles and as part of a strategy for 'more creative and flexible education' (CRE, 2004: 14).

This report has been concerned with distance learning. It is not a panacea for mobile Traveller children, but there is evidence of progress and ICT offers the promise of further enhancement. There is also a strong outreach tradition within TESS, offering bridging with schools but also direct support to Fairground, Circus and Gypsy families in transit. There is scope here for creativity, scope for an approach to mobility which combines the emphasis on school attendance with the strengths of outreach and distance learning but only, as Kiddle has argued, as part of 'a fully professional system' located in a 'national overview of policy' (Kiddle, 1999: 106).

4.1 Moving forward

Attendance legislation for mobile Traveller children dates back to 1908. Compulsory elementary schooling had been introduced through the 1880 Education Act and part of the 1908 Children's Act was concerned to ensure that children received their entitlement to schooling and dealt with school attendance. Section 118 focused specifically on nomadic/vagrant families and, according to Hawes and Perez (1995: 54-56), Clause 3 was specifically added to this Section to protect Traveller families as they had an established pattern of travel for trade or business purposes. The clause outlined a minimum requirement of 200 half-day school attendances during the period October to March, recognising that Traveller communities were normally on the road from April to September. Although timings have been made more flexible this 200 session approach is still the legislative basis of a response to the realities of Traveller mobility and now covers compulsory schooling through to the age of 16. Hawes and Perez argue that this blunt requirement instrument has hardly, if ever, been used in a context where the real challenges have been to break down barriers and establish trust. Guidance from the DfES in 2003, quoted in O'Hanlon and Holmes (2004: 52), similarly urges pragmatism and sensitivity.

However, in practice, the legislation is also understood to mean that when the travelling child is not attending school the responsibility for education rests with the parents, and this leaves TESS working in a grey area. Ofsted has noted something of this dilemma:

> A related issue is the use of distance-learning material for children travelling with their families for mainly work opportunities. Despite some regular en-route teaching support and the maintenance of educational records, this form of provision is not viewed by the DfES as satisfying the requirements for school attendance. If, however, the pupils are registered at a school and attend for 200 half-day sessions, then distance learning can be seen as a support to parents who have the duty to provide the other 180 half-day sessions. The situation represents a dilemma for Traveller education services in that most of the pupils in these circumstances do not make the 200 sessions at school as required, and there is also a question about the use of grant funding to support the education of children for whose education their parents have the direct responsibility for the period in question. (Ofsted 2001, footnote to page 37)

From a grounded perspective the critical question would seem to be how to move from the uneasy situation hidden away in this footnote to a vision of something more visible and effective. The thinking behind the 1908 clause seems to have been to achieve a balance between children's entitlement and practical circumstance, a constructive step in 1908 when access to education equated to school attendance. However, it can be argued that it no longer represents a suitable response within an inclusive policy framework which is intended to embrace difference and diversity. The evolution of distance education has also changed the meaning of educational access and, as the footnote acknowledges, the 200 session target has become impracticable for a large number of mobile Traveller children. From the perspective of both policy and practice there appears to be a need for some rethinking.

The Ofsted comment also highlights the dilemma for many Traveller parents. They choose to travel, many of them for economic reasons and as part of a nomadic tradition which goes back generations. However when committed parents find school attendance impracticable they are not normally making an active choice to take responsibility for suitable home-based EOTAS (Education Otherwise Than At School) under the provisions of Section 7 of the 1996 Education Act. Ironically, it is the families who are most committed to schooling who know their limitations and actively seek support from TESS. Here the issue of 'circumstance' and 'choice' seems critical. Children who are out-of-school and eligible for LEA support for Alternative Provision have an entitlement because of circumstance: for example excluded pupils, children with medical needs, pregnant schoolgirls and school phobics. This raises questions about why Traveller children should still be treated differently, and for Gypsy groupings their treatment may sit uneasily with the amended Race Relations Act. The thinking behind the 1908 balance also seems out of step with a later Children Act (1989), with its emphasis on the best interests of the child. Nor is this just a matter of principle. Entitlement leads to resourcing and this is likely to have influenced the emergence of, for example, ICT-based distance learning approaches. As noted in Section 3, pupil costs for this form of provision are estimated to be approximately £6,000. This compares very favourably with the figures presented in a review of Alternative Provision commissioned by the DfES (TNS Social Research, 2003), where average per-pupil costs for directly managed provision across 60% of LEAs tended to be between £10,000 and £20,000. Kiddle's vision of 'a fully professional system' may well require resourcing driven by some form of entitlement, albeit with new thinking about parental responsibilities and obligations.

An alternative approach

The building blocks of an alternative approach are already evident in practice and noted by Ofsted: distance learning, en-route teaching support from TESS staff, and maintenance and transfer of records. These elements are also evident as part of the European perspective through work encouraged and developed by EFECOT over many years (see for example EFECOT, 1999).

There are also more radical, mobile-school alternatives. The fairground schools of the Netherlands, and the mobile circus schools in parts of Germany and Spain, each reflect an entitlement orientation. Interestingly, English circus proprietors also put their toes in the water some years ago and helped to support four mobile schools. But these were withdrawn following an HMI report welcoming their potential but expressing concerns about inadequacies in resourcing or providing full access to the National Curriculum (DES, 1990). The case for revisiting the mobile school model in the English context has been weakened by significant reductions in the numbers of children travelling with circuses, and with over 200 fairs each week across the UK, the logistics of the English Fairground industry have always been problematic. There are also advantages in a more flexible approach which builds from the legacy of current TESS experience and which has the potential to respond to the fluid travel patterns of many Gypsy families.

From this perspective the question becomes one of using creativity and flexibility to establish a legacy-based framework which could be linked to aspects of entitlement. Here the views of TESS staff, as reflected by discussions within NATT and contributions to the Becta workshops, suggest some useful proposals founded on three premises. First, that base-school attendance and linkage is always to be encouraged. Second, that enhanced (ICT-supported) distance learning is made available to make this link effective, either in terms of direct communication or as part of a blended approach with specialist providers. Finally, that any developments are based on reinforcing a partnership ethos with parents. Their proposals were that:

- Combinations of enhanced distance learning and en-route support should be recognised and adequately resourced as alternative forms of provision where school attendance is likely to be impracticable or inappropriate for any parts of the time a pupil is away from the base-school. The best interests of the child should be the over-riding consideration.

- Attendance requirements should be redrafted in terms of individual learning targets as well as physical presence, with credits for completed units of work as well as actual attendance at base-schools and schools en-route. This approach should be reflected positively in the way base-schools complete attendance records.

- Where appropriate e-attendance, working at set times within an agreed and acceptable distance learning environment, should also be recognised

- Family-held records should be encouraged but should be complemented by nationally agreed and coordinated TESS systems to enable speedy record transfer and the coordination of face-to-face support, and to ensure that children don't fall through the net. A specialised database should be considered. [A similar restricted access database has recently being proposed in Scotland (STEP. 2003: 18]

These suggestions are not definitive but they are intended to establish an enabling vision which can be set against questions about reality. Is it possible to match a more flexible new entitlement with parallel and workable parental obligations to protect the rights of the child? Are there realistic growth points for progress? What are the resource implications? Where do such proposals sit within the reality of the incremental and longer-term process of bridging the divide between the communities and schooling?

Parental obligation

At first sight the current legislation appears to have the benefit of simplicity, at least in terms of enforcement. However apart from the lack of realism about 200 sessions, it would currently be extremely difficult to monitor 'suitable' home-education while families are actually travelling. The abuse of EOTAS is already a serious and increasing concern for TESS, even when working with settled children or encouraging base-school attendance.

The introduction of individual attendance and work targets is not just more viable, it also highlights the importance of drawing parents into partnership, and parental commitment is well documented as critical to effectiveness. Kiddle's text (1999) has a particular focus on the rights and responsibilities of parents as well as the rights of children, and her discussion is rooted in personal experience of mobility, as well as many years as a specialist teacher. The discussion she develops will be familiar to TESS staff, as it recognises the diversity of attitudes and reactions within Traveller communities and in effect confirms the unique role TESS have in establishing a partnership ethos with individual families while also acting as a bridge with schools. Family perspectives are seen to be dynamic, changing over time in the light of new experiences, be they positive or negative. This picture of diversity and change resonates with the findings of the recent longitudinal study (Derrington and Kendall, 2004). New forms of flexible home-school agreement have the potential to be used creatively within a locus of control and partnership. For mobile families committed to schooling they offer a potential structure for systematic support, where the role of parents can be celebrated and training provided. For the more ambivalent they offer opportunities to be used in accordance with the DfES emphasis on pragmatism and sensitivity. For those who might seek to abuse the new framework they offer scope for measurable targets.

4.2 Growth points and divides

The suggestions put forward in this section need to be read alongside the possibilities discussed in Section 3 but, importantly, as part of a longer term process. They cannot address more immediate challenges such as unpredictable departure or families who choose to use periods of mobility to vanish from the schooling map. They need to be seen as part of an enabling ethos which can contribute to a patchwork of incremental change where progress is likely to be based on example and through positive experiences within each Traveller community.

From a national perspective there are more potential growth points within the primary sector. Community commitment to schooling is stronger. Linkage to base-schools is more straightforward and the E-LAMP$_2$ project already points to a new sense of belonging. Where enhanced distance learning is judged as a realistic priority for learning continuity, the school/TESS should explore a suitable (annually reviewed) agreement with the family. If this can be established, resources should be made available and should cover equipment and internet communication costs. They should also be sufficient to cover staffing costs related to the key linkage role during the travel period.

As acknowledged throughout this report, the secondary context is more challenging. Where there is scope for current base-schools to support existing learners the support could and should be enabled in the same way. Further consideration also needs to be given to piloting the integrated LEA and/or regional models described in Section 3. These are more suitable for families who are away from base for long periods and there will be important practical lessons to be learned, not least about new forms of partnership with base-schools. There are clearly some pupils who would benefit. Some have developed a degree of self-study skills and are motivated and supported by their parents in working towards Key Stage 4 qualifications however great the challenge, as evidenced by the two pupils now using email in Hertfordshire. There are other children from committed families who have progressed well at primary school but give up in the face of the practical difficulties posed by the secondary phase.

However, for the longer term, and for the majority of Traveller children, it also seems clear that there are fundamental issues concerning distance learning which are inseparable from broader questions about the perceived relevance of secondary education, the responsiveness of schools, school attendance and the range of concerns which Traveller parents express. The curriculum perspective needs to be understood in the broader sense as '… the social process that animates and gives meaning …' (James *et al*, 1998: 41). From this perspective the reality of the educational curriculum of the Traveller home, be it Gypsy or Fairground, is very different from that of school. As Holmes and her co-authors note:

> The travelling communities historically have sought to be self sufficient, independent and resourceful. They have largely operated in extended family groups providing a mobile workforce and/or organising around … business interest(s) … Child rearing practices and skills have focused on children as trainee adults learning alongside adults and being inducted into the family work from a young age (11/12 years old). Strong family education and work skills have been transferred from generation to generation in this way, ensuring continuity of the community and its work traditions. (Holmes *et al*, 2001: 75)

The gulf they illustrate resonates with one of Kiddle's chapter titles, 'Between Two Worlds', and with the work of authors such as Kenny (1997) who have focused on boundary issues from the perspective of ethnic identity. In the distance learning context, the periods when school attendance is not a realistic option, the learner is arguably even more firmly immersed in the educational curriculum of the home. For most secondary-age Traveller children, a distance learning approach built on the positive aspects of informal apprenticeship and role models, and with the involvement of parents, seems far more likely to be successful than an attempted extension of school programmes. What does seem clear is that any attempt to offer effective distance learning for disaffected Traveller pupils, or pupils within disaffected families, is likely to require the full measure of flexibility and creativity recommended by the Commission for Racial Equality.

Where children are actually attending school and are mobile for relatively short periods, datacard communication could support the kind of relevant project-based activity which is already characteristic of best TESS practice. Creative use of enhanced communication could even play a part in reinforcing home-school links. Where the concern is for families who travel away for substantial parts of the school year, any potential progress seems likely to require a more radical approach which starts with the realities of the home curriculum and builds on intrinsic motivation. Here the constructivist approach which characterises Notschool.net offers important insights, with its stress on learning through 'meaning making' rather than through syllabus-led 'knowledge transmission' (Jonassen and Land, 2000: iii-ix). Such approaches are possible and the experience of Notschool.net suggests that they can be successful in terms of learning objectives which include formal accreditation. However, depending on how great the gulf is, they raise fundamental questions about the role and capacity of secondary base-schools and differing perspectives on the 'best interests' of Traveller children over time. These considerations require broader judgements which were felt to be outside the scope of the current project.

In concluding it seems important to return to the underlying threads which run through this section. The emphasis has been on creating an enabling and entitlement ethos for distance learning within an approach which also recognises the importance of encouraging school attendance en-route, outreach work and record keeping; each as parts of the overall response to different patterns of Traveller mobility. The current E-LAMP$_2$ survey suggests that the vast majority of services outside the Greater London area are supporting children with either distance or independent learning packs in numbers varying from a handful to about one hundred. This suggests that responses of this kind are an important option. TESS vary in size and structure and this may affect their current capacity to support distance learning developments. New ICT-based approaches may have both direct and indirect resource implications. Levels of progress with and within base-schools are also likely to be a significant factor. On the other hand there are something like 1200 children with existing packs, which suggests the potential for immediate growth points, particularly in the primary sector and currently with a bias towards the Fairground and Circus communities. It is also important to acknowledge the additional challenges of the secondary sector. Where these are logistical this report has argued for a pragmatic approach, reinforcing work with some base-schools and exploring the blended use of specialist distance learning providers. Where they are related to the divergence between home and school there is scope for creativity but any radical alternative would need to be considered within a framework of broader policy objectives.

Notes

[1] The Showmen's Guild of Great Britain is the main trade organisation for the Fairground or 'Show' community

[2] Niner has suggested a related need for additional LEA base pitches for between 1,000 and 2,000 families (See ODPM, 2003)

[3] Resolutions 89/C 153/01, and 89/C 153/02 of the European Council and Ministers of Education meeting within the Council. The 'Occupational' grouping includes the Fairground and Circus communities.

[4] This survey is being undertaken as part of the follow up E-LAMP$_2$ project. It is hoped that the full results of the exercise will be available in October, 2004

[5] North East Lincolnshire and five London LEAs had no current TESS structure or coverage. The London authorities were Barking and Dagenham, Islington, Wandsworth, Westminster and City of London.

[6] 'New Opportunities Fund' ICT training was a major initiative to support all schools. LEAs had discretion to include central teams, like TESS. Additional funding was subsequently provided to ensure that the needs of support services for children with medical needs were addressed, but TESS were still not included.

[7] A series of projects was coordinated by the European Federation for the Education of the Children of Occupational Travellers (EFECOT) during the period 1996-2000. The most significant were TOPILOT, FLEX and Trapeze. For an overview see Marks (2003).

[8] Vu2 Media Ltd is also piloting 'Vu2learn' which is intended to support learning at home for primary age pupils, with timetabled internet broadcasts and follow up activities. However this service is currently designed for reinforcement: to support children who are regularly attending school or whose parents have taken the full responsibility for home learning. The service requires a 'broadband' connection.

[9] GPRS is a system especially designed to transmit data, rather than voice, traffic over mobile phone networks. It also has the advantage that it doesn't automatically loose a connection when the signal becomes too weak, an all too familiar problem for mobile phone users.

[10] Interim feedback is based on a tutor workshop and responses from eight parents, together with a variety of comments from pupils. The full evaluation of the trials will take place in the autumn.

References

Bhopal, K., Gundara, J., Jones, C., and Owen, C. (2000) *Working Towards Inclusive Education: Aspects of good practice for Gypsy Traveller pupils* DfEE, London

Bhopal, K. (2004) Gypsy Travellers in Education: Changing needs and changing perceptions *British Journal of Educational Studies* Vol 52(1) 47-64

Chen, Y-J (2001) Transactional distance in world wide web learning environments *Innovations in Education and Teaching International* Vol 38 (4) 327-337

Central Advisory Council for Education (1967) *Children and their Primary Schools (The Plowden Report)* HMSO, London

CRE (2004) *Gypsies and Travellers: A strategy for the CRE, 2004–2007* Commission for Racial Equality, London

Danaher, P.A. (2000) Guest editor's introduction *International Journal for Educational Research* Vol 33 (3) 221-230)

Derrington, C and Kendall, S (2004) *Gypsy Traveller Students in Secondary Schools: culture, identity and achievement* Trentham Books, Stoke on Trent

DES (1990) *A Survey of Four Mobile Circus Schools: A report by HMI* DES, London

DfES (2003) *Aiming High: Raising the Achievement of Gypsy Traveller Pupils* DfES, London

DfES (2003a) *On the Move: Managing Pupil Mobility (Guidance)* DfES, London

DfES (2203b) *On the Move: Managing pupil mobility: (A handbook for induction mentors)* DfES, London

Dobson, J.M., Henthorne, K. and Lynas, Z. (2000) *Pupil Mobility in Schools: Final Report* Migration Research Unit, UCL, London

Duckworth, J (2003) *Evaluation of the Notschool.net Research Project: Phase III pilot 2003* [Report available from Notschool.net, Ultralab, Colchester]

Durham and Darlington TES (2001) *Effective independent learning in the primary school* [available from the service]

EFECOT (1994) *What is your School Doing for Travelling Children: a guide to equal opportunities through distance learning* EFECOT, Brussels

EFECOT (1999) *Travelling on Together: 10 years EFECOT* EFECOT, Brussels

Elen J (1996) Didactical aspect of self-study material In de Volder M.(ed) *From Penny Post to Information Superhighway: Open and distance learning in close up* Uitgeverij Acco, Leuven

Evans (1992) Preface to the English Edition, in Centre for Gypsy Research *The Education of Gypsy and Traveller Children* University of Hertfordshire Press, Hatfield

Hawes, D and Perez, B (1995) *The Gypsy and the State: The ethnic cleansing of British society* SAUS Publications, The University of Bristol

Holmes P., Knaepkens L. and Marks K. (2001) Fighting Social Exclusion through ODL: the development of initiatives with the children of Traveller communities, in Trindade A.R.(ed) *New Learning*, Universidade Aberta (Portugal): pps 74-86

James, A., Jenks C., and Prout, A. (1998) *Theorizing Childhood* Polity Press, Cambridge.

Jonassen D.H., Peck, K.L. and Wilson, B.G. (1999) *Learning with Technology: A constructivist perspective* Prentice Hall, New Jersey, USA

Jonassen, D.H. and Land, S.M.(eds) (2000) Preface *Theoretical Foundations of learning Environments* Lawrence Erlbaum Associates, London

Kenny, M. (1997) *The Routes of Resistance: Travellers and secondary level schooling* Ashgate, Aldershot.

Kiddle, C. (1999) *Traveller Children: A voice for themselves* Jessica Kingsley, London

Liégeois, J.P. (1998) *School Provisions for Ethnic Minorities: The Gypsy Paradigm*, Hatfield, University of Hertfordshire Press.

Marks, K. (2003) EFECOT: Supporting the Travelling Tradition, in Bradley J.(ed) *The Open Classroom: distance learning in and out of schools* Kogan Page, London pps 67-83

Meadows, P. and Stockdale, K. (2003) *To raise the achievement of Traveller pupils at The John Warner School through using ICT in Distance Learning*, Hertfordshire Traveller Education Project and The John Warner School.

Moore, M.G. (1993) Theory of Transactional Distance in Keegan, D (ed) *Theoretical Principles of Distance Education* Routledge, London pps 22-38

Niner, P. (2003) *Local Authority Gypsy/Traveller Sites in England* The Office of the Deputy Prime Minister, London.

Notschool.net (2003) *Summary of Research Findings Phase 3: A vision of future learning* Ultralab, Anglia Polytechnic University, Chelmsford

ODPM (2003) *Local Authority Gypsy/Traveller Sites in England: Housing Research Summary Number 195* The Office of the Deputy Prime Minister, London.

Ofsted (2001) *Managing Support for the Attainment of Pupils from Minority Ethnic Groups* Ofsted, London

O'Hanlon, C. and Holmes, P. (2004) *The Education of Gypsy and Traveller Children: towards inclusion and educational achievement* Trentham Books, Stoke on Trent

STEP (2003) *Inclusive Educational Approaches for Gypsies and Travellers* Learning and Teaching Scotland, Glasgow.

TNS Social Research (2003) *Survey of Alternative Provision 2003: Research Report* TNS, Richmond, Surrey.

Vanbuel, M., Marks, K. and Reynolds, S. (2000) *The Trapeze Project: Supplementary project report* [This unpublished document can be made available via one of the original project partners 'ATiT' email: atit@atit.be]